A GIFT FOR

_____

PRESENTED BY

_____

THE AWAKENING
of The Universal Mind

A Collection of Poems, Affirmations,
Quotes, and Activities

Shireen Violett

Volume II

BALBOA
PRESS
A DIVISION OF HAY HOUSE

Copyright © 2016 Shireen Violett.

All rights reserved. No part of this book may be used or reproduced by any means, graphic, electronic, or mechanical, including photocopying, recording, taping or by any information storage retrieval system without the written permission of the author except in the case of brief quotations embodied in critical articles and reviews.

Balboa Press books may be ordered through booksellers or by contacting:

Balboa Press
A Division of Hay House
1663 Liberty Drive
Bloomington, IN 47403
www.balboapress.com
1 (877) 407-4847

Because of the dynamic nature of the Internet, any web addresses or links contained in this book may have changed since publication and may no longer be valid. The views expressed in this work are solely those of the author and do not necessarily reflect the views of the publisher, and the publisher hereby disclaims any responsibility for them.

The author of this book does not dispense medical advice or prescribe the use of any technique as a form of treatment for physical, emotional, or medical problems without the advice of a physician, either directly or indirectly. The intent of the author is only to offer information of a general nature to help you in your quest for emotional and spiritual well-being. In the event you use any of the information in this book for yourself, which is your constitutional right, the author and the publisher assume no responsibility for your actions.

Any people depicted in stock imagery provided by Thinkstock are models, and such images are being used for illustrative purposes only. Certain stock imagery © Thinkstock.

Print information available on the last page.

ISBN: 978-1-5043-6055-5 (sc)
ISBN: 978-1-5043-6057-9 (hc)
ISBN: 978-1-5043-6056-2 (e)

Library of Congress Control Number: 2016910678

Balboa Press rev. date: 09/06/2016

Book also written by Shireen Violett

"I AM" In "My Right Mind"

Acknowledgements

This book is in gratitude to "I AM" and to all those beautiful beings who have participated in my life and have given me opportunities for personal growth, development, and discovering the many possibilities in understanding our Oneness. From the depth of my Heart, I am forever grateful to my family and the One Most High—Thank you, Thank you, Thank you.

Blessings, Love & Light—"I Am" Shireen Violett.

Keynote

This book is written for *all people of the world*. Its message is inclusive and for all who care to understand our Divine Uniqueness in this world and how we co-create our own reality to serve a "Higher Purpose" and connect with All That Is.

Keywords are written in *capital letters, bold words, bigger fonts, quotations and sometimes smaller italicized words* to energize the reader. These emphasized words are meant to resonate with the reader, create a *transformation* and strike a chord of *remembrance of who we are (part of a greater whole),* and to help us recognize that our Oneness is based on our knowledge of our spiritual journey and our Soul's need to connect on all levels of our Being.

Contents

Heaven On Earth	1
I Believe	3
Someone	5
Meditation	7
The Blue Man	9
Thought	11
SEVEN	13
Mind	15
Extraordinary	17
OM	19
CHAKRAS	21
Angel Wings	23
LIFE	25
There Was a Time	27
One Moment in…Our Love	29
Forgiveness	31
The Eye of God	33
The Colors of Love	35
The Door of Opportunity	37
Freedom	39
Harmony	41
Perfection	44
H O P E	47
Attitude	49
I AM Only in Your Eyes	51
That's ALL I Have to Say	53

Mission and Vision Statement

To always be the best that I can *BE*, using my creative talents and the knowledge of the Mind, Body and Spirit to create a higher level of *Conscious Awareness* using "Creative Thought & Art" to express "Words of Wisdom" that expand the Heart and sustain the desired life, causing the "Doors of Opportunity" to open and connect with All That Is. Thus allowing one to experience *Love,* the transcendental nature of our true essence, the Authentic Self, encouraging our Spirit to connect on all levels of existence, experiencing Oneness and bringing about a *Transformational Shift* from *within* creating *Knowledge, Wisdom and Inspiration* for all who want to know and feel the *true powers* of "**I AM**."

Poets utter great and wise things which they do not themselves understand.

—Plato

Prologue

These transformational writings are meant to inspire all those who are Mindful of the world we live in, and those who recognize that Mindful Science is important in the world of transformation. These individuals who know this realize from their Intuitive Inner Guidance and hard work that we must focus on ourselves and our mental capabilities from *within* to connect with our Spiritual, Physical, Mental and Emotional worlds in order to become successful and co-create the world we desire to live in.

In my previous book, *"I AM" In "My Right Mind,"* I felt the need to express the wonderful experience of just being human and loving the *magical, mystical,* and *spiritual* parts of ourselves. I wanted to convey that as we evolve and grow, and we learn to *love* ourselves more, we are able to connect with our Higher Self (thus giving us the opportunity to use more of our right brain—trusting ourselves more intuitively). And as we learn how to use this *gift* more, we learn to trust our true nature and live in a world of *gratitude* at how fantastic our Creator is in giving us so much to fill our minds with—so many wonderful opportunities to learn, grow and build upon.

There are so many wonderful individuals in our world who are teaching us helpful ways to think about how we create in life, (e.g., self-help books, art, music, retreats, wellness centers, wellness cruises, documentaries, workshops, and seminars). My hope is by using Creative Art in the form of *written* and *spoken word*, my readers will be *empowered* to think in a creative way using these transformational verses to expand and sustain the desired results they are striving to manifest. *"Creative Thought"* is very *Spiritual;* it brings much *Joy, Love* and *Peace* to the Mind.

My poems are about *inspiring, informing,* and *transforming* what is truly a gift: this magical school of life. The poems are also spiritual, mystical and transcendental. They are *the Open Door* for the readers to search for *words, titles* and *unfamiliar terms* that he/she may not be aware of, or might not have given much thought to in the past. For example, my poems speak a lot on the subject of M*indful Science,* showing how mental our world actually is. It is essential to know that *Sound* and *Vibration* work together in unison to create the world we live in.

According to Metaphysics and Quantum Science, we are like magnets, attracting all that we desire according to our *vibrational level. This information is important* because according to the Law of Attraction, we receive all that our attention is set upon. Therefore, it would be very beneficial to focus on having a higher vibration to attract and manifest perfection in our lives. When we speak, we are using Sound to implement the words and thoughts of our Minds. We are creating actions through words that cause reactions which affect our daily lives.

This is where *Creative Art or Mental Art* comes into play. You are encouraged to use "mental transmutation" to change the undesirable circumstances in your life to desirable conditions using positive awareness and affirmations. This is achieved by learning and using the *Universal Laws* that govern our world. My poems are filled with positive *Affirmations,* reminders of *Universal Laws, Words of Wisdom* and *encouragement* to learn more about life (e.g., *Chakras, Meditation* and *Creative Thought*).

We are a Unit of One, a Unity of Greatness, and when we believe in ourselves and our abilities to supersede the shackles of our past, we are able to co-create with All That Is and live a life of beauty, wonder, and fulfillment that encourages *Our Minds Consciously and Constantly* to *BE Constructive* and *Creative*.

This creative work of art speaks to the *Heart, Mind* and *Spirit* of the individuals who are searching for Truth, Honor and Love—those who can feel and know that we are so much more than these physical bodies that we wear.

Readers are encouraged to search *within* and look everywhere possible for confirmation of something greater than the status quo, something that is magical, mystical, and unique and might just possibly be staring right at you.

It is essential to *look within* ourselves and use the powerful tools available to us, such as *Prayer, Meditation* and *Affirmations*. These three forms of *creative spiritual awareness* are *sure to make a formula for success when used with sincerity, repetition,* and *stated as a fact* (that is as if it has already happened) in the quest for knowledge and a desired outcome.

The inspirational writings in this book ensure we know just how special life is. When we rehearse beautiful words of wisdom, we live our truth and we know that we are *Love* (which is the highest form of energy). We create the Peace, Love and Harmony that we seek when we *raise our vibration* and rise above the status quo.

We are not limited in our world to create; we are only limited by our thoughts to create. We are more than you can ever imagine. *Individually*, we are a *Microcosm* (a smaller part of the Universe), however, *collectively* we are a *Macrocosm* (a bigger part of the Universe). That is to say, "We are One," a major part of the Whole. In other words, everything in existence matters —*all the pieces of the puzzle are important whether great or small,* the flap of a butterfly wing affects all.

Thank you for taking this *sacred interpersonal journey within* with me and allowing *The Doors of Opportunity* to open.

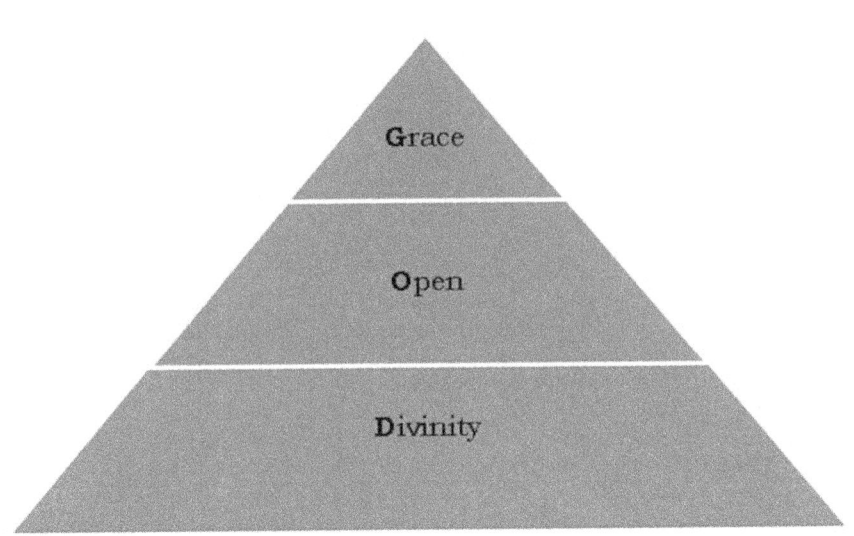

The most beautiful thing we can experience is the mysterious. It is the source of all true art and science.

—*Albert Einstein*

Heaven On Earth

I look into my Source's Inner Eye, and I see something right here on Earth that's Sacred and Divine. I'm looking through the Heart of His creation and I see the *Trees*, the *Flowers*, the *Bees* and the *Butterflies* at ease, just hanging around near the rivers and the seas.

There is new life everywhere. I see the *Lotus* flower with its Sacred Pure Heart and Mind; the *Lily* with its Chastity, Dignity and Innocence; and the *Rose* with its Love and Beauty. Each is promising a new birth, a transformation, and a new beginning—a brand new day.

And as I *look within*, I see all of these creations singing out loud. *Look inside*! See the greatness and the grand scheme of All That Is—Life as a Mystery, Mystical and Beautiful, *ONE times One Hundred and Forty-four Thousand.*

Look at you.
Look at me and All that exists,
a marvelous creation of wonder
"I AM" *Three times Three* "I Am."

What a King of kings, a Master of masters, a Creator that's *Unlimited, All-knowing and Everywhere* at once. A Creator who has created Life as a *Moment of Wonder*, giving me something I can feel, touch, and see. The signs of His Love are everywhere I put my attention and let my *Heart Open*. *This must be it*, what those great Saints and Adepts have been saying all along. This is it, a brand new day—*Heaven on Earth.*

All that we are is the result of what we have thought.
—*Buddha*

I Believe

The Universe is perfect, and so are we. It matters not who is right or who is wrong. What really matters are the choices that we make in life—not the end of the journey, but the footsteps we take along the way.

It matters not who created the issue, but how can we solve it? We may ponder at why it was created and, if anything, what are the possibilities of common ground. If we see it as an *opportunity* to learn and grow, then we've "*mastered the game of life.*"

If we see the challenges in our life as something to be fearful of and decide to retreat, then we haven't yet learned how to *open our hearts and master our Minds* to find the answers for growth and development.

We are like magnets and our choices affect our lives every moment, every second, every day, and in every way we are blessed to breathe in "*the gift of life.*"

After all, didn't someone say that "knowledge is power"?

How else would we learn but through our experiences? How do we gain that *power within* without taking the higher ground? It is only by knowing *"I AM" Love—The Higher Me.*

I AM That I AM, co-creating my life everyday—my reality, giving me the perfect opportunity to express life and gain my freedom, realizing that this is a perfect world—and I'm living as *I Believe.*

The minute I heard my first love story I started looking for you, not knowing how blind that was. Lovers don't finally meet somewhere, they're in each other all along.

—*Rumi*

Someone

I woke up this morning feeling so exhilarated. Why had the Angels touched my Soul this day? I could sense them in their Etheric Bodies of Light. Why were they singing *"Wake up and pray, wake up and pray, for now there is a new love in your life this day"*? "See him," they say, "in your *Inner Vision*. See how lovely he is in his Body of Light, shining with bright, sparkling, colors."

>See how much he Adores your Soul.
>See how he sends you *waves* and *waves*
>of the *Heart Energy* to the core of your Being.
>He embodies "*The Christ Consciousness.*"
>He knows the powers of all "I AM."

His vibrational sound waves are like music in my ears. He is the One who has made my Heart *Open* and *Expand* to the beauty of The All-knowing, The *LOVING ONE,* and The Divine. Source of my life. And as my Heart is squeezed one last time, and I feel the powers of all "I AM," my Soul sings:

>*A love so sweet and ever Divine*
>Holy, Holy, Holy

>A Love that gets better and better with time
>and the power of prayer. And then it hit me—
>my aha moment, my epiphany—I realized that
>my Creator had sent me—*Someone.*

Close both eyes to see with the other eye.

—*Rumi*

Meditation

I wish you could see me now, in my folded-leg position.
I am flying, twisting, and turning in the Tunnel
of Life, deep in the Universal Mind, "I AM."

These are my most precious moments, I am having the greatest time of my life with the One Most High. I'm in the most beautiful and sacred place that takes me higher and higher as I go *within*. I'm quickly realizing that in order to see change, a **M**odification of my daily life is necessary. The more I *change* my outlook on life, the more **E**nlightened I become about myself and the world around me.

This beautiful, loving, sacred place *within* is **D**ivine. It is a gift for those who take the time to go into a quiet place and **I**magine that our world is perfect. I do this by choosing positive **T**hought. I'm only focusing my attention on creating an attitude where I look at the possibilities of all my life issues.

As I look daily *within* my Inner Vision, I feel myself **A**scending to a higher level of awareness, a place where I **T**rust the Universe and know that all is as it should be. It's challenging me to think greater and better ideas (looking outside the box) so that my consciousness, the **I**ntuitive part of me, the authentic me, *illumines* the world I live in.

I feel the **O**neness in all that is created. My life is filled with **N**irvana—a peacefulness and a blissfulness that no other gratification in this life can compare with its sacredness. The gains that await us are unlimited. It's so amazing to sit and have an *inner* conversation with yourself, a *love affair* with Spirit, *a union of the Heart*, a quietness, a stillness, a moment of Thought and Gratitude—***Meditation***.

Love has no desire but to fulfill itself. To melt and be like a running brook that sings it's melody to the night. To wake at dawn with a winged heart and give thanks for another day of loving.

—Kahlil Gibran

The Blue Man

Oh, yes, you'll know him when you see him; he's always kind, loving, and ever so gracious. His *Energy* can be felt a mile away. His Heart cries of the "*Christ Consciousness*" everywhere he interacts and resides. He's sure of himself, and he knows how to challenge your Soul (that is your Higher Self).

He'll make you work for his Vibrational Love, the kind of Love that you never want to be without. He'll challenge your Mind and make you think of *Heaven.*

He'll get right into the center

of your *Seven*

and shake your world until

you surrender.

And when you look in his Mind, in his Inner-Eye, and you see *shooting stars, floating hearts and rainbows of energy* flying all over the place, you'll know that

he's got your power,

because he opened

your Flower and now

he's your Rising Sun.

He's from the Seventh Ray. He's that *Sapphire* you Love, the Violet Flame's sacred gift—***The Blue Man.***

That a man can change himself, improve himself, recreate himself, control his environment, and master his own destiny is the conclusion of every mind who is wide-awake to the power of right thought in constructive action.

—Christain D.Larson

Thought

Someone planned *human life* with great precision

BE

Food	Social Skills
Shelter	Mental Reasoning
Clothing	Community
Family	Variety of Cultures

LOVE   COEXIST   WORK

What if there were "No Thought" in life?
No Order,
No Reasoning,
No Mental Mind,
No Law of Attraction bringing us
the experiences we need,
no diversity—
everything is the same,
no Love at all.
Would we then feel life had abandoned its purpose?

EVOLVE

When we look around our world and see the beauty of each day, we see order in day and night, order in the seasons and life itself. We see order in the sun, the moon and the stars, and our solar system. We know that life it is built on **M**ental **T**hought which is **C**reative, **C**onstructive and **S**piritual, a sacred gift in the Mind of God—*Thought*.

The principles of Truth are Seven; he who knows these, understandingly, possesses the Magic Key before whose touch all the Doors of the Temple fly open.

—The Kybalion

SEVEN

My eyes are opening now and I see the number Seven. I am a prisoner of its energy, I capitulate (surrender) to its charm. I am captivated by its Sacred Geometry, the luckiest number in Heaven.

Seven has captured my Mind, Heart and Soul because "I AM" *Seven times Seven,* and "I Am" ready for *Eleven,* the Master Number that vibrates with Heaven.

"I AM" Seven and "I Am" awakening.

Seven Spinning Wheels of Life
Seven Levels of Heaven
Seven Bodies Unveiled
Seven Universal Laws

This is the Secret to life, The Law of Attraction, the *SEVEN* highly effective habits of "I AM."

Thought
Creativity
Harmony
Balance
Charity
Grace
Love

These are the activities of "Universal Mind" that will make my life function like Heaven—the mystical number—*SEVEN.*

To a mind that is still, the whole universe surrenders.

—*Tao Tzu*

Miracles

Innate

Nature   IS

Dynamic.

MIND is **ALL** There Is—**GOD** in Action—*Universal* M I N D.

Mental

Intellect   IS

Now

Divine.

To change your world, you must change your vibration.

— *Florence Scovel Shinn*

Extraordinary

Energy
Xtra-special
Thought
Radiant
Art
Omnipresence
Renaissance
Divine
Imagination
Nirvana
Ascending
Reasoning
You

I see the Infinite in these mystical words—it's that magical number *Eight*. I see the *shape of life transforming* as a beautiful *work of Art* in each and every one of these old perennial words. Just sit back and imagine how wonderful you feel as you repeat these words of *Love*. It's all you are, all you know, and all you'll ever need and more. ***You*** are the Love and Light of this world—*You are Extraordinary*.

Science is not only compatible with spirituality; it is a profound source of spirituality.

—*Carl Sagan*

OM

Can you hear it?

–*OM*–

How *sweet* the sound.

How Holy Thou Art in Thought.

–*OM*–

"I AM" the World you see—the Cosmos, the Universe, the Ethers, the Moon, the Stars, the Sun, the animate and the inanimate, the Birds, the Flowers, the Trees, the Oceans and the Seas.

BE   –*OM*–

Oh rise, ye, all Creatures, and all Life Forms of the Angelic and Elemental realm. Oh rise, ye, all Life Forces, all Mankind, the seen and unseen, the known and the unknown—in all the beautiful forms of **"I AM."**

I see a great work of Art in All That Is.

Universal Mind Creating Perfection,
Unlimited, All Knowing and Everywhere at once,
Beautiful, Glorified, Love, and Light…*OM*.

When the kundalini rises you have to learn something new to ride the serpent.

—Shireen Violett

CHAKRAS

Life is a gift and "I Am" Conscious that this is my Heaven right here and now. I know that this opening in my life is a privilege and a birthright, *looking within* my Being to know who "I AM."

My Heart *is opening* and I'm now co-creating with All That Is. I feel the Kundalini Energy moving up and down my spine. It's Rising up and singing in a vibrational sound. It's time to Ascend to a higher level of awareness and let the Serpent ride.

It's ready to Open New Doors,

to let your sun, the rising star, shine on those invisible things that twist and turn: the Seven Spinning Wheels of Life—*Chakras.*

The energy of the mind is the essence of life.

—Aristotle

Angel Wings

Every day I thank my Divine Source for my *Invisible Body of Etheric* Light and my *Invisible Wings* from the One Most High. I know these things exist because when I meditate I'm flying and communicating with my Source from *within* the corridors of my *Inner Mind,* that world which is beyond the physical realm...

As I let go of the outside world, I am feeling myself twisting and turning while I *go within.* I'm going deep into the Tunnel of Life, moving in a guided way with precision *to the Light.* And as I relax, I am gaining a huge insight to my *Inner World*— a glorious path, a magnificent *right-of-way,* a gateway to Enlightenment for those who are open to *Inner Sight.*

My Crystallized Eye has finally opened and I am truly amazed and in awe at how Beautiful and Mystical this Inner World is to my *outer reality*. I realize that more work is needed, on my part, to explore and soar with my new found freedom. After all, I could go to places no Being has ever known. I could find the answers to all my questions. I could travel to those places that have held some of life's deepest mysteries. I might even seek out my A*kashic Records*—after all I am free to open my Mind to Higher Realities. I could even, *Mindfully,* connect with my *Higher Self* and ask for specific instructions regarding my physical environment in the "here and now."

It just seems that the *possibilities* are *so many*—no limitations when I sit quietly in my *sacred space*. Perhaps I will just fly off, somewhere into no man's land, and I'll meet you there when we've both *mastered our lives* here in this physical realm.

Here is what I do know about this reality: there are no limitations when I'm *looking within* my Soul's Inner Eye. It's our Soul's gift to our Spirit to fly with the One Most High. Thank you, Divine Source, for my *Angel Wings.*

Life is a mission, not a career. A mission is a cause. A mission asks, "How can I make a difference?"

—Sean Covey

LIFE

Life is just like going to the movies.
LET THERE BE LIGHT—

Ready,
Set,
Action,
Possibilities, Opportunities, and Freewill—
Life Imitating Life

Just like Nelson Mandela, I'm taking charge of my Mind: *I'm not a victim.* I am the master of my fate; I know how to create with the infinite number *Eight.*

I'm working hard to improve my conditions wherever I am, and I'm teaching myself and the world *how to Love,* not to hate. When I start working on me, *looking within,* the rest will follow—it's never too late.

I play with all the tools available to my Mind: people, places, books and things. The world is my playground and I'm good at my game.

Mahatma Gandhi, Pope Francis and Martin Luther King, Jr. were all good at making us look at our shame, and showing us how to be thoughtful masters of the game.

Life, Life, give me my *time,* give me my *plots,* give me my *play,* and let me receive the blessings and assistance of the Chohan of the Seventh Ray, using the Mighty Violet Consuming Flame "I AM."

Tick tock, tick tock, while time moves on…we watch you rock, and we wait for you to return back home to the Etheric Realm, and tell us how you created Conscious Awareness during your brief stay, while on the clock…tick tock, tick tock, in a perfect world…**C U T**—*Life.*

Your living is determined not so much by what life brings to you as by the attitude you bring to life, not so much by what happens to you as by the way your mind looks at what happens.

—*Kahlil Gibran*

There Was a Time

You know that something really great has happened when you feel worthy of life. You no longer think, *How can I?* You know with conviction, *Yes, I can*!

Yes, I can live in my Heart each day the sun shines. I can co-create the perfect world in a place where I live as I believe—a place where *"I Am" Christ Conscious*, a place where my Heart speaks, a place where I no longer look at the other person for the answers, but I *look within* my own eyes, my inner self, my inner vision, a place where my "I AM" Presence lives, showing me a world that's very unique and Divine.

You see, I don't worry about what others may do, think, or say. I focus on my own reactions to *life's gifts* and *possibilities*, learning how to grow up and be wise. You see, I've stopped that drama long ago—feeling that I'm the victim, that I am not worthy and things will never change.

Well, let's just say ☺ I've done something wonderful with myself. *I have changed my approach to life* and the way I use to think about the challenges in my life, and now I'm on the other side of life—**Serving, Giving, Receiving and Co-creating** with **All That Is**.

I *don't attract those negative things anymore.* I've got a new walk, a new way in my life. I've got my groove back now—"I walk the talk." And so, when you see me with my new swag and all—and if you must know, I got my mojo back in the fall—and now you see me standing tall. You might have said this about me before, my *conscious effort to awaken* and *change within*. I didn't know myself at all—*There Was a Time.*

Love is a symbol of eternity, it wipes out all sense of time, destroying all memory of a beginning and all fear of an end.

—Madame De Stael

One Moment in…Our Love

I sleep so beautifully, and when I awaken in a lucid state, I see *Our Love* in His Eyes, *Our Movements* in His Eyes, *Our Moments* in His Eyes. I see *Our Hearts* in His Heart—I see the "*Colors of Love*" together in a Heart Shape—Purple, Pink, and Magenta. I see whirls and whirls, spirals and spirals of Cosmic Energy.

> I see your Heart—*His Heart*;
> I see your Love—*His Love*;
> I hear your Tune—*His Tune*;
> I sang your Song—*His Song*.
> His Love, His World—His manifestation of who "I AM,"
> His manifestation of who we are, *His gift to those who are consciously aware of His living existence in their Secret Chambers*—His Heart filled with Love as we dance and swirl
> One Moment in Time—**One Moment in Our Love.**

Without inner peace, outer peace is impossible.

—14 Dalai Lama

Forgiveness

I am asking you to forgive me because I
did not recognize who you were.
Forgive me when I looked you in your eyes and
had thoughts that were less than perfect.
Forgive me because I did not recognize you were
giving me the opportunities I needed for growth.
Forgive me because I failed to recognize in myself the
powers of "I AM" and that I actually have *freewill* to
do greater and better things in my life each day.
Forgive me because I failed to realize that
I am not a victim but I am co-creator of
my world. I'm the master of my fate.
Forgive me, my friend, because now when I see you,
I see myself—we are One and the Same,
just different aspects
of life.
And now with *Love*, I forgive myself
because I know in this moment that I do
have the ability to *correct my thinking* and know that the
Real Power in life is *"No Judgment"*
but *"Forgiveness."*

It is the secret of the world that all things subsist and do not die, but only retire a little from sight and afterward return again.

—Ralph Waldo Emerson

The Eye of God

I woke up this morning and I heard someone say
"get up, pray, and meditate."
Look inside of your inner world.

And there He was, this Beautiful, Glorified Presence showing me a world that is truly amazing and ever so Divine. And what a magnificent sight to see, an amalgamate of colors so richly defined—Purples, Pinks, Blues and Magentas *so deep in clouds of Love.* I see Great Divine Beings who are wearing robes of bright, sparkling colors, whose loving presence is just so awesome=cheering me on, letting me know I am not alone.

They are telling me to realize that *"I Am"* co-creating my reality with Him and it's now time to manifest these realizations in the physical realm.

Under Grace,
"I AM" Hope,
"I AM" Faith,
"I AM" Loving Charity,
"I AM" Joy and Happiness,
"I AM" Peace and "I AM" Love.
I see myself and our world, and I know without a doubt,
"I Am" Perfect in *The Eye of God.*

Love is composed of a single soul inhabiting two bodies.

—Aristotle

The Colors of Love

I look into your eyes, and I see the symbols of
our hearts, 🫶
two beautiful beings looking deep into the Soul.
I see something that says
"I AM" the Colors of Love;
"I AM" the rainbows in their full height;
"I AM" Purple, Pink, Magenta, Teal and Blue;
"I AM" all the colors of you;
"I AM" the Secret to Success;
"I AM" the Law of Attraction,
The Axiom of Love,
"I AM" that deep feeling of bliss
when I hold you tight in my Heart,
"Pink on Pink, Blue on Blue."
I feel Love all over me,
and when I look in your eyes,
I see all "I AM," I see—*The Colors of Love.*

What lies behind us and what lies before us are tiny matters compared to what lies within us.

—*Ralph Waldo Emerson*

The Door of Opportunity

I sit so very quietly and I *look within* at what has to be the most beautiful, serene place I've ever had the pleasure to be in: my temple, my kingdom, my inner world, the place where the One Most High awaits my arrival and greets me with showers of Love.

I rehearse this ritual daily, and each time a little more is revealed. Sometimes I just go out on a whim, looking at galaxies and things to come, the colors, so rich and intricately defined, a symbol of power, our Source in action.

Beautiful Holograms in their Etheric Bodies of Light are telling me, "This is your Heaven right here and now. Welcome, dear beloved one, we've waited for you for so long. Look at this beautiful place, *The Open Door*, where Mystics, Ascended Masters, and Prophets have come to sit and recline for a while. No one knows how far you've traveled. No one knows how much you've unraveled as you look at the complexities of life."

And as I quietly sit and withdraw my Mind, I'm comforted by the thought that Grace gives me the tools to use *within*, to *Visualize the Possibilities and Solutions*

to what may appear impossible, but to the one who goes deep within— this is

The Door of Opportunity.

Your work is to discover your world and then with all your heart give yourself to it.

—The Buddha

Freedom

Just listen to these words and see how far they carry you—all the way down into Egypt. I hear the cries of "Let my people go." It is one of those great tales that oscillates way down into the soul. We are meant to be on this journey to release ourselves and our foes from tyranny and confusion, inside and outside.

In our Minds, we must say *"no"* to the *oppressor*, heavily invested into ego. It's time to realize that all people must be **F**ree to honor and respect the true authentic self. To the *oppressed*, we must let go of fear and say, "No more shackles on our feet or intellect, internally or externally."

We are now ready to *take action* and **R**esponsibility for ourselves. We are ready to use our Minds to **E**volve and **E**nlighten ourselves. We are ready to invest in who we are, taking charge and taking the higher ground, "walking the talk," and remembering in our subconscious mind that we are **D**ivine Beings having a human moment, and that our Source is creative and **O**mnipotent. Every soul must have its challenges in order to grow and expand—nothing is static.

And now without a moment of hesitation, we are ready to take some quiet time to *look within* and **M**editate—a quietness and a stillness that's worth more than gold, places or things—worth more than anything a man might give his soul, an innate involution of the spirit, rising up vertically and evolving as the kundalini energy, the rising serpent, creating a mystical *phenomenon inside*, giving you the right to know who you are and how you shall go forward in life on this spiritual journey.

I have a dream that all who read these sacred words will one day experience what I mean.

How *sweet* is the sound of the Universe

—OM—

Freedom.

Enlightenment is absolute cooperation with the inevitable.

—Anthony de Mello

Heaven
Attention
Reflection
Meditation
Omnipotence
Nirvana
You

These words are the *Music of Life*.
They reflect the Oneness of All That Is.
All creation must work together to create
this Sacred Agreement in life—
The Law of Correspondence,
a Harmonic Accord,
Harmony.

You can't teach a man anything, you can help him discover it in himself.

—Galileo

Perfection

Is it something to strive for, or is it you, or me, or the White Golden Light on a brand new day, or those phenomenal Rainbow Rays that lay hidden in the sky on a hazy night? Or is it the Sun, the Moon and the Stars creating night and day in the same equal length in a grand equinox way

Or

perhaps it's the vastness of the Adriatic Sea and all it serves on an average day, or all the deep blue oceans and seas combined with their hidden treasures challenging you—if you are brave enough to ride the waves and take a deep-sea peek

Or

it might possibly be that beautiful cat in the alley with its tiger-like stripes and deep blue slit-like eyes, or man's best friend who is always just a bark away, looking after our homes with such glee, or just another sunny day in the month of June

Or

maybe, it's Yao Ming, who is a little more than seven feet tall, shooting hoops in every hall, bringing our *awareness to nature* and how she calls our minds to be aware of our *animal kingdom*, or the two little red-headed boys, Javier and Reese, playing dodge ball in middle school with their snotty noses and curly toes, or it just might be that little black boy, De'Jon, with one blue eye and one brown eye that nature gave him as a gift so unique—just try to imagine how exceptional he is

Or

perhaps, it's those big black and white whales in the sea—the most beautiful Orcas that we are privileged to see, nature's most prized gift in the sea of life. All they need for us to do is honor their space and let them live freely as they give us a treat. They are teaching us how to use our *Spiritual Minds*, just as they use *Sonar Sound Waves* and *Vibrations— echolocation*—to communicate with other life forms. Observing and working with these beautiful creatures urges us to work more with our *Inner Guiding System*—which connects us to the higher spiritual realms when we are *consciously aware* of how our *brain waves* (beta, alpha, theta, delta and gamma) work to increase our intuitive knowledge and spiritual awareness, we gain control of our lives.

I think I know what perfection is. I think I've got it. It's all the Life Force that exists in the heavens and the earth, all that makes up our entire Universe, the Cosmos, the minute: mesons, quarks, gluons, corpuscles, atoms, molecules, cells, electrons, protons, the smallest, the biggest, the least, the greatest; the All-Knowing—creating the most unique and mystical world, seen and unseen, known and unknown. "As above, so below, as below, so above." We are perfect—*Mind, Energy,* and *Matter* at its greatest: Divine *Perfection.*

Hope sees the invisible, feels the intangible and achieves the impossible.

—Helen Keller

HOPE

There is a Crystal Cord, a vessel of Sacred Energy that cradles the Heart, moving up, in, around, and through our Bodies of Light. It is a gift of nature to envision ourselves and our world as we desire it to be, and so it must be.

Imagine a world without Heaven,

without Opportunities,

without Peace

without Eternal Life,

the ultimate gift of Grace for hard work, sacrifice, trials, and tribulations is that we grow and learn to Love Him,

"The One"

who creates and co-creates

with our Minds, teaching us that we do have the power to *look within* and be amazed by our acts of creation—so diverse, so beautifully defined—life with so many twists and turns,

a Spiral of Energy,

life so pure, so gracious, so sacred,

a Holy Grail of Cosmic Energy,

The Universal Mind

of *Hope.*

The greatest discovery of any generation is that a human being can alter his life by altering his attitude.

—William James

Attitude

Yin and Yang, Oh Great, Yang and Yin, Source of the Feminine and Masculine Energies, show me: What are the *actions* of a Divine Mind, a Spiritual Being, who desires a successful life in the physical, mental, and spiritual realms of existence—one who wishes to create a space of no pain? Tell me the greatest *secret* of all: using the Law of Attraction on how to win the Game of Life and feel no shame.

All
Transformation
Thoughtful
Imaginative
Truthful
Unity
Divine
Enlightenment
These words all add up to equal one big word:
LOVE
When you have this ingredient inside and out,
the world belongs to you.
What do you think of these wise words:
"TO BE OR NOT TO BE?"
I heard someone say
"The difference between winners and losers
is *ATTITUDE.*"

Who looks outside dreams, who looks inside awakes.

—Carl Jung

I AM Only in Your Eyes

My Heart, Mind and Soul tell me that my *inner strength* lies in my ability to *know* and *recognize* that *Spirit* is *Love*.

So I sit quietly in my little space and I dream of Him in my Secret Chambers, knowing that he'll come to me and he'll give me a little squeeze and a whole lot of Love, if I just sit for a moment and *look within*.

> Oh, what a beautiful Mind I have—
> God so Loving and full of Grace,
> so very Perfect in my eyes,
> *a glow of pink mist*
> changing into Symbols of Hearts
> and Words of Love.

My heart just melts so profoundly with joy because I knew He would come and take me to far distances, to places beyond my knowledge, and show me a world that's very Divine.

I am now captivated and I'm in His eyes and I'm feeling so fine. I'm caught in His Mind. He knows how much I love His designs, my life is filled with so much *Love* for something that's greater than wine. I love my time with Him because He shows me a world that's destined to be mine, and He promises me if I work hard every day to seek Him *within*, I'll never know anything greater than His *Love*, His *Heart*, His *Words*. He whispers to me, *"I AM Only in Your Eyes."*

When it is darkest, men see the stars.

—Ralph Waldo Emerson

That's ALL I Have to Say

I am knowing and feeling that something amazing is stirring within me, through me, and outside of my Being, and it's greater than anything I've ever imagined.

It has a grip on my *Heart*, my *Soul*, my *Mind*, and my being. Its Light is so strong and powerful but yet so gentle. It wants me to know.

"I,"
"I AM,"
"I AM" Seven,
"I AM" Awakening,
"I AM" Realizing Him,

that Golden Light, and the opportunity to join Him and know the realization of "I AM."

I'm rising, I'm falling, I'm blazing in His Light. He moves up, in, around and through me as I learn how to fight. I'm no longer in anarchy, superstition, and voodoo's sight.

I work in the Light

I see the wonders of a heavenly night. I'm ascending in my own right. I know it now—I realize it now, that we are One in this Great Body of Life. We are stars shining ever so bright—*star light, star light*, won't you shine in my Heart tonight?

I hear the sound of …OM…*far and near*. I hear the words "in the beginning was the Word, and the Word was with God, and the Word was GOD"—*That's ALL I have to say*.

Epilogue

The seeds of perennial wisdom have been planted, and now you will go out and make a difference in your life and the world you have created collectively. It's time to keep those promises from eons of time long ago, to all those around you, as you aspire to *open* your *heart* and *mind* to a higher purpose.

My hope is that your goal will be to never stop searching for the truth, never to accept the concept that it can't be done. I hope that you will push the limits of *Mindful Science* from a Spiritual, Mental, Physical and Emotional level and know that this is nature's special gift to you—to discover the real you, the authentic you.

Furthermore, I hope these transformational writings have inspired you enough to realize that we are the masters of our world. We co-create it every day, and it is of the utmost importance that we are *consciously aware* of the *Natural Laws of Spirit*. It is the only way to move forward and shoot for the stars and beyond. In other words, we must always be Constructive and Creative in mapping out our lives.

And finally, the poems in this book can be used as *tools for growth* and *self-development*. The purpose of this book is to *think, create, and jot down* your inner most feelings and thoughts (poems or affirmations). Feel free and have fun with the new creative you; after all this is your divine birthright, your inheritance to peace of mind, health, abundance, and the power to control your destiny.

The Heart is the key to "I AM."

PART II

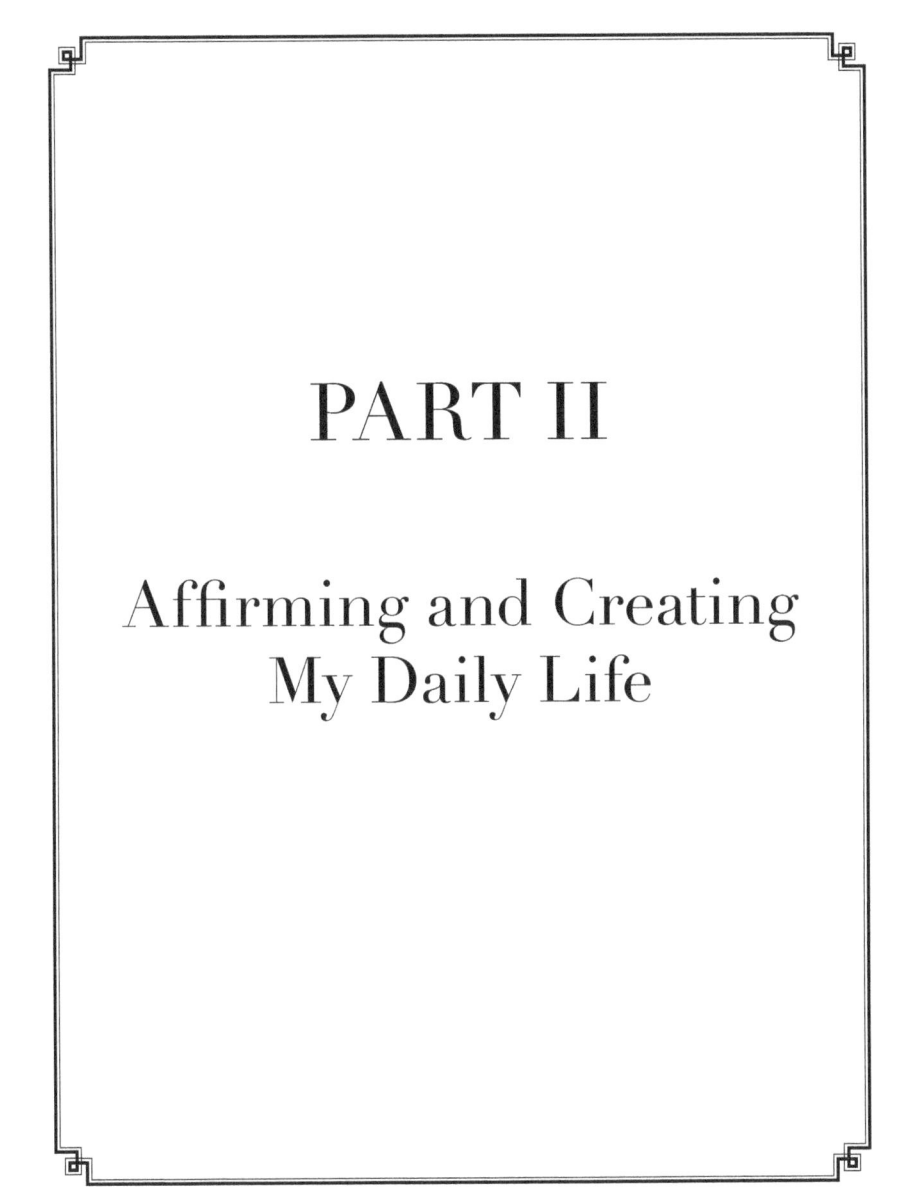

Affirming and Creating My Daily Life

Everyone thinks of changing the world, but no one thinks of changing himself.

—Leo Tolstoy

Rewards of Affirmations

In my previous book, "I AM" in "My Right Mind," I listed twenty-six affirmations with minimal detail. In this new work, I am giving more detailed information explaining the benefits of using and learning more about affirmations. Some may ask: What are affirmations? How do they work? Why are they necessary?

Affirmations are positive Mind Treatments. They are about *change*. They can and do work on a Mental, Spiritual, Physical, and Emotional level. They are able to shape your future in positive ways, especially if they are repeated on a daily basis with sincerity and your attention is focused on the outcome—in other words, it is a *fact*, you already have what you need.

According to Mindful Science and Quantum Physics, we are like magnets—affirmations work well with the Law of Attraction (also known as the Law of Supply). When you create your own affirmations, you are *consciously* cocreating your life; you are attracting what you need. You are taking charge and being responsible for your life. Thoughts and words become things as you *visualize* yourself whole, healthy, and perfect.

The affirmations that I have listed are just the tip of the iceberg. You can create your own and as many as you like, or use the ones that are listed. You can meditate on them, sleep on them, and create with them in any way you feel comfortable that will help you receive the full benefits of positive action. Always create your affirmations as a fact—such as, "I AM whole, healthy and perfect."

I use them in my writings because they are positive Mind Treatments and Transformational in nature. When used consistently, they create and attract what you need. Using the treatments everyday by reading them out loud will work on a *vibrational level*, attracting what you need, bringing harmony, peace of mind, and creativity into your life. In a sense this *empowers* you, finally letting you take charge of who you are and giving you the choice to create what you desire.

I strongly recommend that whenever you have an uncomfortable situation, get out a pen and paper. Always remember—the way of the Masters is *transmutation* (the process of changing the way you think) not denial. Start writing positive affirmations that *attract favorable conditions* into your life. Be Creative and Constructive. Have fun!

Daily Affirmations for the Mind, Body & Spirit

AFFIRMATIONS

Open

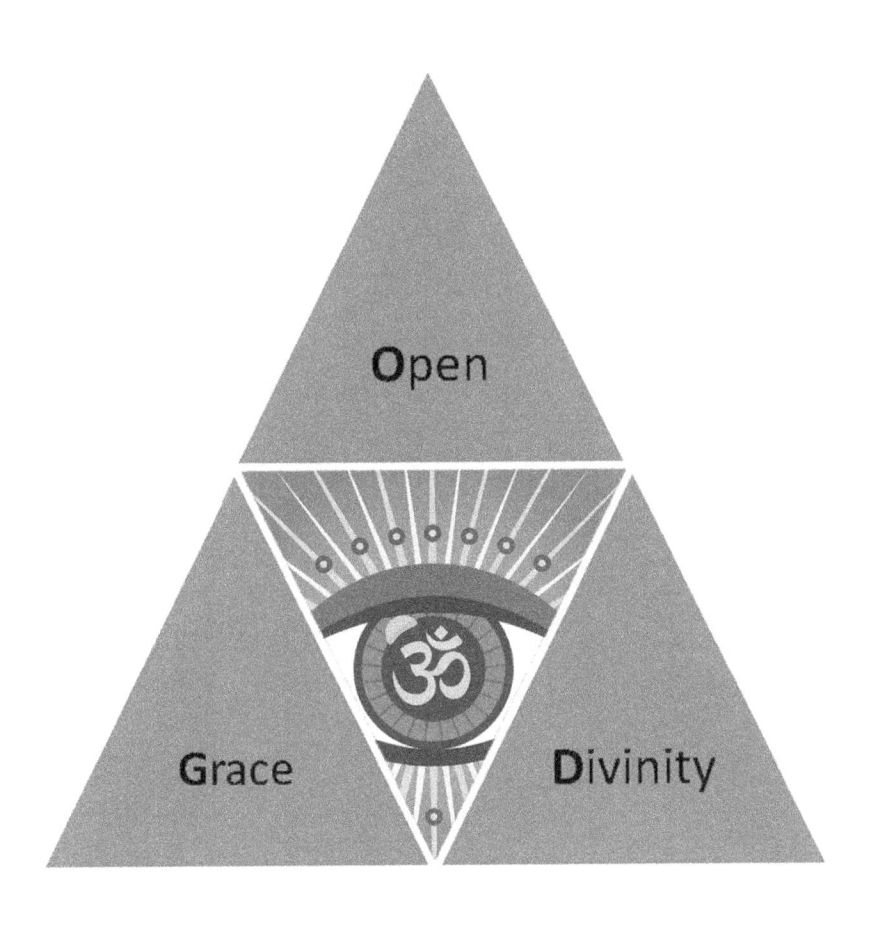

Grace **D**ivinity

I AM grateful for this moment that is Now.

I AM the change I seek.

I AM the Love I desire.

I AM open for new opportunities.

I AM the gift of Charity.

I AM always positive.

I AM intuitive; I listen internally.

I AM thankful for my daily experiences.

I AM Whole and Healthy.

I AM always fulfilled in my Heart's desire.

I AM Prosperous.

I AM always Expanding and Evolving.

I AM Beautiful.

I AM One with All That Is.

I AM Successful.

I AM Worthy.

I AM Protected by the Divine White Light.

I AM Happy.

I AM always *Learning* and *Teaching* better ways to enjoy the journey of life.

I AM Committed to Daily Journaling.

I AM a Vehicle for Spirit.

I AM the Open Door.

I AM Love & Light.

I AM Perfect.

I Love Myself.

"I AM" in "My Right Mind."

```
        Mind
    "I AM"
Heart       Soul
```

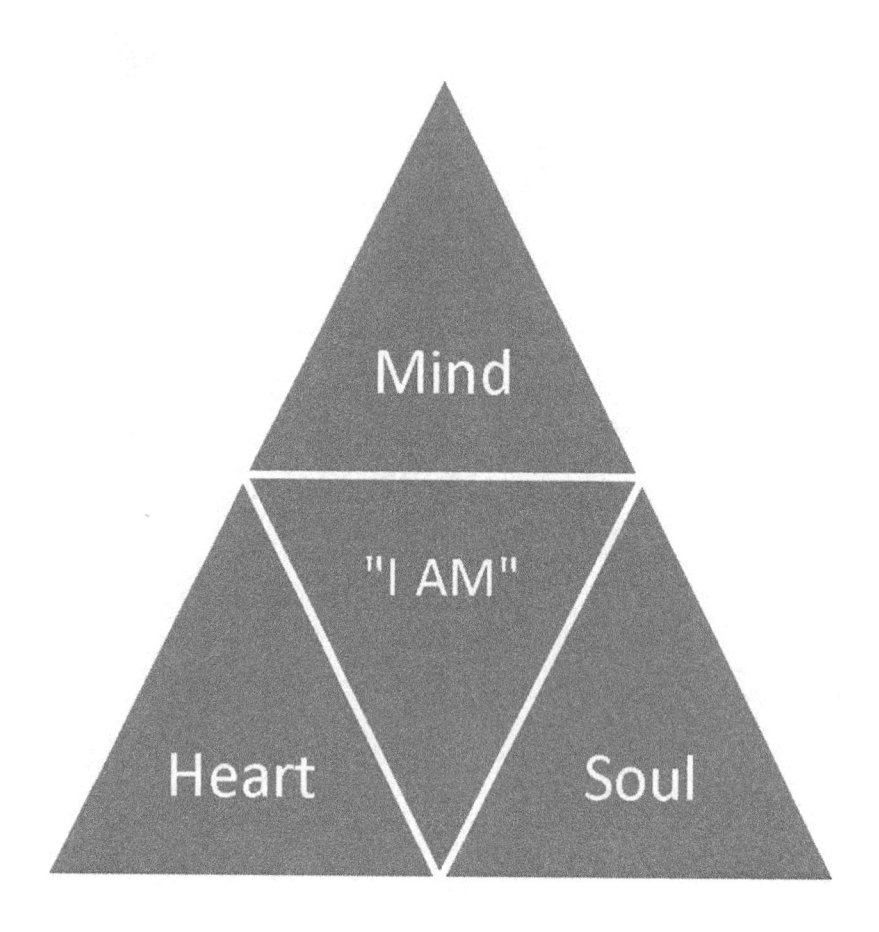

The Last Word

You have the ability to choose to be whatever you desire. If you think about creating a world that is filled with Hope, then there is *only one* gift to give to yourself and our world, there's only *one vibration* to attract. You decide.

Live		Failed
Open-minded		Ego
	versus	
Very		Against
Enlightened		Reasoning

You can **Mindfully** decide

Love   or   Fear

"You Have Freewill."

PART III

Creating Purpose, Awareness, Focus, Action, Transformation & Empowerment

Workbook

Learning and knowing about these *Sacred Centers* are essential to a perfect Mind, Body, and Spiritual Self-Realization.

Be in *harmony* with *yourself*

Through these centers pass energy of an extraordinary kind, whose versatility and vitality opens the gates of consciousness to undreamed-of opportunities and realizations.

—Flower A. Newhouse & Stephen Isaac

Create your own *Mission* and *Vision* Statement.

Create your own *Mission* and *Vision* Statement.

Create your own *Mission* and *Vision* Statement.

Create your own *Poems* or *Inspirations*.

Create your own *Poems* or *Inspirations*.

Create your own *Poems* or *Inspirations*.

Create your own *Affirmations*.

Create your own *Affirmations*.

Create your own *Affirmations*.

Take *notes* on your favorite *Poems* and *Affirmations*.

Take *notes* on your favorite *Poems* and *Affirmations*.

Take *notes* on your favorite *Poems* and *Affirmations*.

Have a look at the beautiful *Zen Garden* on the opposite page; sit back and relax; *Dream* and *Meditate* on it, envision all the beautiful colors you might like to add to this *holistic garden* as you personalize it and make it your own.

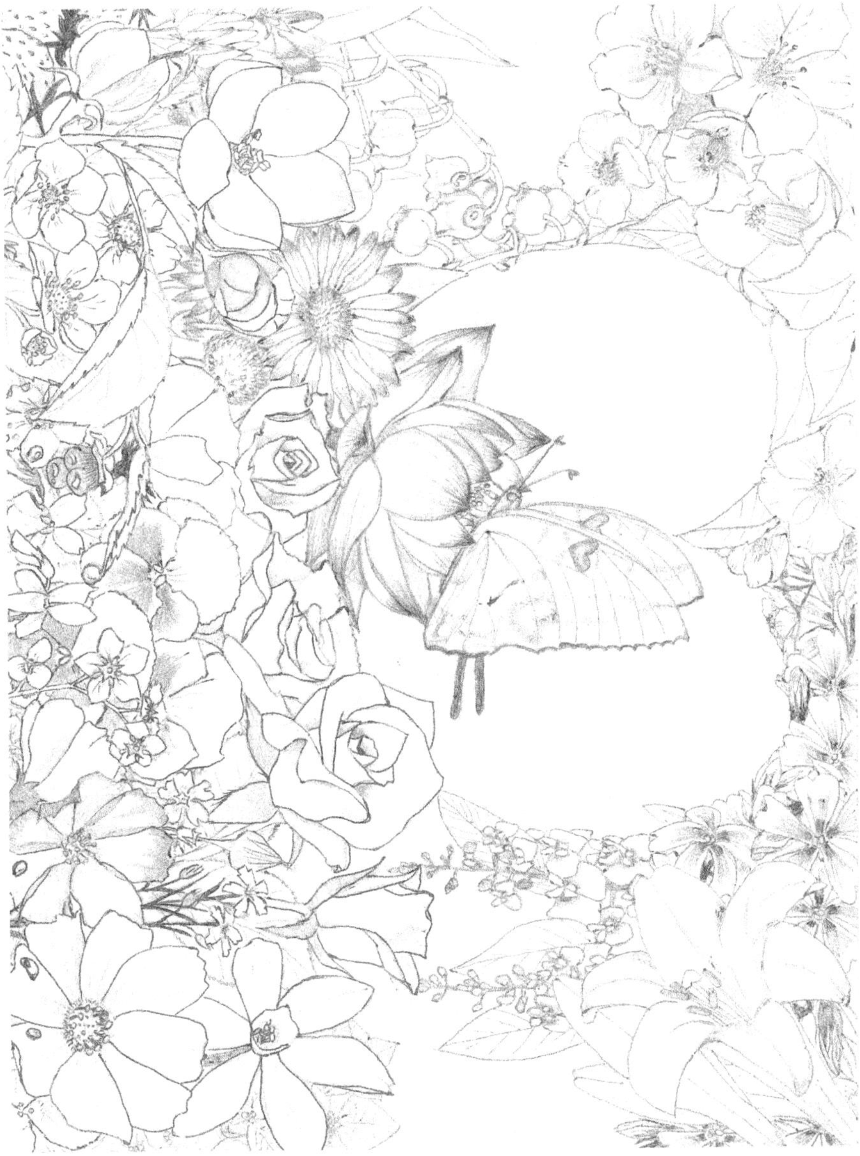

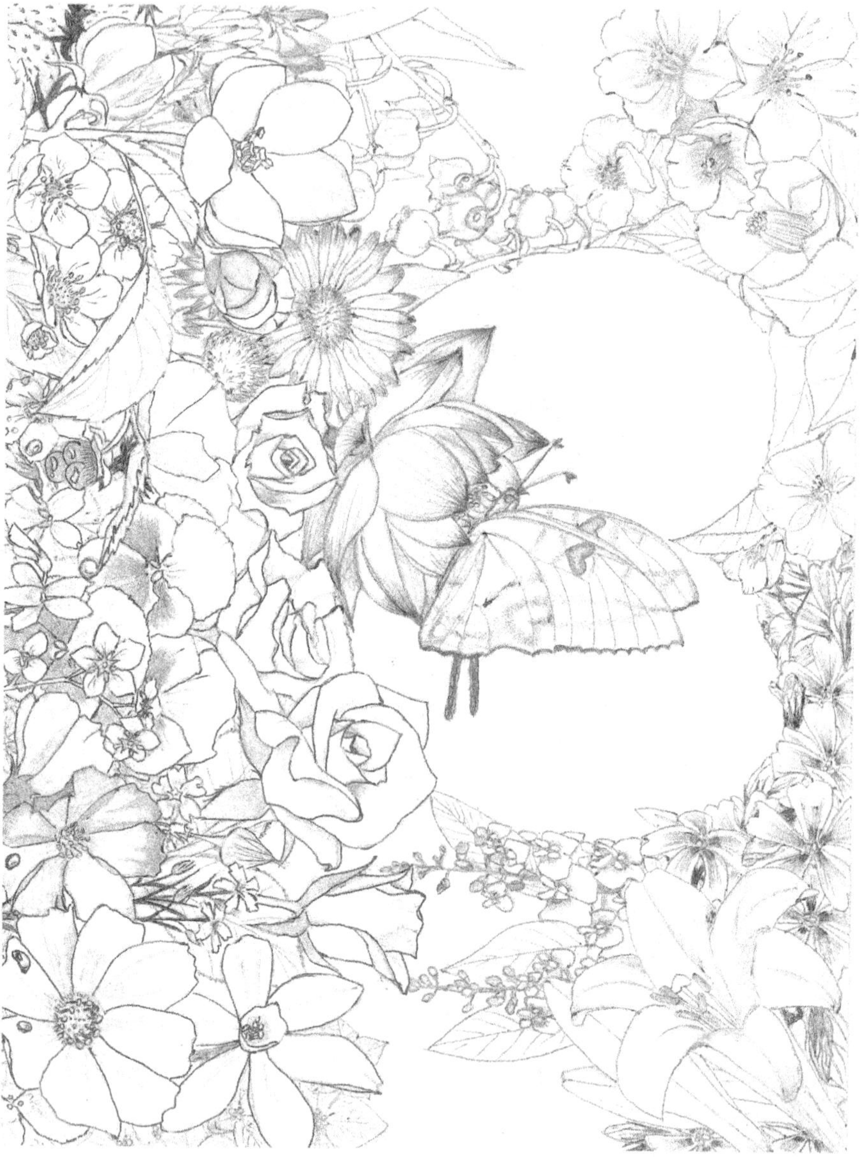

115

Having some knowledge about this vast subject, *The Platonic Symbols* and *The Seed/Flower of Life* is a gift to anyone who wishes to expand in their spiritual growth and self-development. Study it, draw it, mediate on it and sleep on it. The *benefits* are enormous.

METATRON'S CUBE

METATRON'S CUBE

METATRON'S CUBE

Visualize and *Meditate* on this *Zen Heart*; personalize it and make it your own.

Visualize and *Meditate* on this *Zen Heart*;
personalize it and make it your own.

Visualize and *Meditate* on this *Zen Heart*;
personalize it and make it your own.

Visualize and *Meditate* on this *Zen Heart*;
personalize it and make it your own.

Create your own *Zen Garden* or *Zen Doodling*.

Create your own *Zen Garden* or *Zen Doodling*.

Create your own *Zen Garden* or *Zen Doodling*.

Coming Soon

* * * *

"I AM"
In
My Heart

A Collection of Poems, Affirmations,
Quotes, and Activities

Shireen Violett

Volume III

On the following pages is a *preview* of excerpts from the author's next book of *Poetic Inspirations*.

I AM in Love

There's something wonderful and mystical happening in my life. I am having a *renaissance* with myself, a feeling of knowing. There's a deep mystical knowledge in the core of my Sacred Heart, an *Involution* and *Evolution* occurring simultaneously, something magical that's hidden deep in my Divine Blue Print. It's something that my Soul has been preparing for from eons of time gone by.

I feel it—it's him, that gifted Spiritual Being. I know it. There's a Lover in my Heart—a Cosmic Avatar, a Divine Being who has worked very hard to be there in that *etheric space*. He knows I am here, I am ready, I am *open* to him. I feel the rhythm and vibrations of *Love*.

Each time he holds my Heart, I die a thousand deaths; and each time he seizes my Mind, my Soul recreates a new me; and each time I rise out of the ashes like the Sacred Phoenix, I am experiencing a *Rebirth* and a *Transformation*, I am feeling like a new virgin (untouched) every time I see him in my *inner vision*. I am *visualizing* a strong, thoughtful, Christ-Conscious Being, wrapped in drapes of Cobalt Blue, a conscious-minded Lover knowing how to entertain my Mind, my Heart, and my Soul, reminding me of a *Force* that is greater than any physical mind can imagine, encouraging me to *look within* and just *allow* for the *Joy* and *Love* of two Hearts synchronizing with Him—

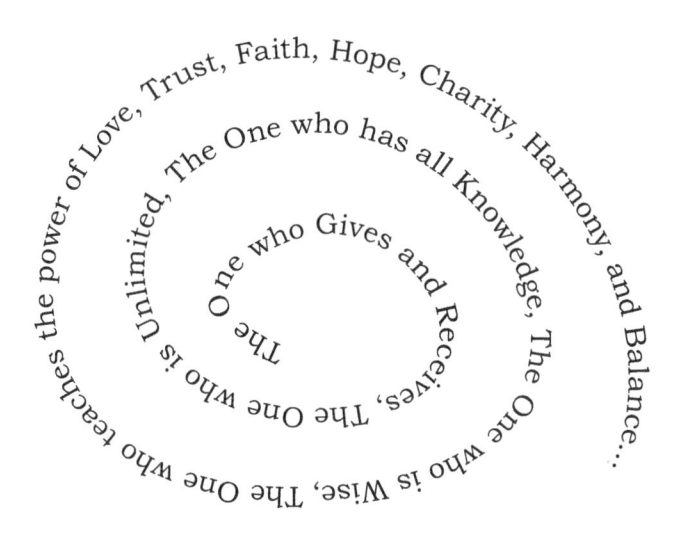

...teaches the power of Love, Trust, Faith, Hope, Charity, Harmony, and Balance... Unlimited, The One who has all Knowledge, The One who Gives and Receives, The One who is Wise, The One who is

and gives us our well-earned life with the one who deserves our open-minded likeness, one who is vibrationally drawn to our conscious awareness through his *electronic, magnetic mind*—his highly evolved soul and our mutual interest of the *Sacred Heart* guides us to what one famous poet intuitively knew and stated many years ago:

> *"Lovers don't finally meet somewhere; they're in each other all along."*

And as I lie here in my reflective state, seeing my *Energetic Flame*, the one who ignites my Heart, my Mind and my Soul, I know without a doubt...***I AM in Love.***

I Can Do It

As I sit quietly and contemplate my life, closing my eyes, inhaling and exhaling, releasing old paradigms of the past—*negative thought patterns:* fear, unworthiness, lack, poverty and pain—voices telling me no, no, no, it's someone else's fault not mine…and then I hear it ever so quietly in my mind…and I feel it, my Adonai, my Lord, whispering—go ahead and let it go—break the shackles of the past from your feet. Loosen the grip of *"I can't"* and "this is the way we've always done it" from your mind.

Spirit has my attention now, and I'm a little more inclined to sit back and recline while my Soul rehearses memories long forgotten. Up to this moment of darkness I have felt alone, but now my helper, that *inner voice*, reminds me that I was never alone. It was I who made the choice to go it on my own before the big bang theory and the arrival of dawn.

My Higher Self reminds me of my origins, and I see it—my place, my kingdom, my glorified home, and I suddenly know from *deep within*, I am more than this shadowy frame I wear, I am more like the "Violet Flame." I've just figured out a way to overcome this game.

No more "Dark Nights," I've won the right to be who "I Am"— mindful, thoughtful, creative and "the effect." I am no longer frozen. I know how to create with the Infinite Eight, I've torn down the barriers that caused me to regret. I'm that incredible Divine Spark that knows who "I AM"—

"I AM" Love,
"I AM" Light,
"I AM" This and I "AM" That,
"I AM" All I choose to Be

And I am right to chase the stars to their full height and beyond, working with the Universal Mind into the middle of the night to gain my intuitive gifts, my *birthright* to seek, until my *Inner Eye* opens with *Sight*.

I finally understand, this journey is all about me—learning how to trust the Highest Part of Me, knowing who "I AM." And now "I AM" taking charge of my Mind—and the *Light* comes in, up, around, and through me, and I know LIFE: Yes—*I Can Do It*.

FINIS

About The Author

Shireen Violett is a Metaphysics Educational Counselor, a Mystic Poet and Empowerment Coach. She is a life-long student of Metaphysics. She is presently living in Florida after many years abroad.

Shireen enjoys participating in charity and gala events where she is a licensed Metaphysical Healing Practitioner—practicing Intuitive Mind-Body Medicine (Energy Healing) and Therapeutic Touch. She is also available to read her Inspirational Writings, give lectures, and lead seminars and workshops on *The Art of Mindful Science, I AM Awakening, The Art of Conscious Awareness Using Poetry, and The Art of Poetry*.

If you have enjoyed any Poem or Inspirational Thought in particular, and you would like to contact the author via email, please feel free to send inquiries to shireenviolett@hotmail.com.